Antarctic Penguins

Alan Parker and Catherine Parker

Contents

Penguins	2
Emperor penguins	4
Adélie penguins	5
Surviving in the Antarctic	6
Catching food underwater	8
Emperor penguins and chicks	10
Adélie penguins and chicks	12
Penguins' enemies	14
Where emperor and Adélie penguins live	16

Penguins

Penguins are birds of the southern oceans. There are no penguins in the north of the world.

Penguins cannot fly. When they come ashore, they stand upright on their short legs, and take small, waddling steps.

Adélie penguins

Penguins have flippers instead of wings. The flippers are like paddles, and they are the perfect shape for swimming. Penguins are excellent swimmers. They look as if they are flying underwater.

Like all birds, penguins are covered in feathers. They have dark heads and backs, and white fronts. Penguins have short tails and thick webbed feet with claws.

There are 17 different sorts of penguins. Two kinds that live and breed in the freezing Antarctic are the emperor penguin and the Adélie penguin.

Emperor penguin

Adélie penguin

Which penguins live and breed in the Antarctic?

Emperor penguins

- Emperor penguins are the tallest penguins of all. They grow about a metre high.

- They have a yellow patch of feathers on their necks.

- They care for their eggs on the pack ice, and do not make nests. They do not sit on their eggs, but keep them warm on their feet.

Emperor penguins and Adélie penguins live and breed in the Antarctic.

Adélie penguins

- Adélie penguins are smaller. They are two-thirds the height of emperor penguins.

- They have white rings around their eyes.

- They sit on their eggs in nests made of small stones. They nest on stony ground.

Which penguins have white rings around their eyes?

Surviving in the Antarctic

For much of the long Antarctic winter, the sun does not rise at all. Icy gales blow most of the time. The temperature drops well below freezing and stays there.

Few living things can survive — but some penguins can. Male emperor penguins stand on the Antarctic pack ice for the whole of the winter!

To help keep out the cold, penguins have a thick layer of fat, called blubber, under their skin.

A fluffy layer of soft feathers grows close to their skin, and their top feathers overlap like roof tiles. These make a thick, waterproof coat.

Adélie penguins have white rings around their eyes.

To survive blizzards, emperor penguins huddle together in large, circling groups to keep warm. They take it in turn to act as windbreaks on the cold, outer side of the group. Then they slowly move into the middle of the huddle to get warm again.

There is no shelter on the pack ice, so the emperor penguins shelter each other.

How do emperor penguins help each other to keep warm?

Catching food underwater

Penguins catch their food in the ocean. Some penguins can stay at sea for months.

Adélie penguins

Emperor penguins help each other to keep warm by huddling together in large groups.

Penguins breathe and rest on the surface of the sea. Then they dive down to catch krill (which are small animals like shrimps), fish and squid.

Adélie penguins and emperor penguins usually dive for about six minutes at a time. Emperor penguins dive the deepest. They can sometimes stay under water for nearly 20 minutes.

Penguins have a streamlined shape, and swim by making powerful strokes with their flippers. They use their feet and tails as rudders, and they can twist and turn as they chase their prey. They can see fish in dark water.

Penguins catch their food in their sharp beaks and swallow it underwater.

What do penguins catch?

Emperor penguins and chicks

Emperor penguins crowd together onto the Antarctic pack ice in winter. Each female lays one egg. Then she goes out to sea to feed, while her mate takes care of it. He has to carry the egg on his feet. He keeps it warm, under his feathers, for nine weeks! All through the black midwinter days, the male cannot eat.

Penguins catch krill, fish and squid.

After spending the winter at sea, the well-fed female returns with her stomach full of fish and krill, and brings up this food for the new chick. At last the male can go back to the sea to feed. The female warms the chick on **her** feet until he comes back with more food. Then they change over.

At six weeks old, the chick is big enough to be left with other chicks to huddle in a crèche, while both parents hunt for food.

When chicks are six months old, they have their adult feathers, and they can dive to catch their own fish and krill.

Where do male emperor penguins spend the winter?

Adélie penguins and chicks

Adélie penguins breed in summer in large groups called rookeries. They build nests of stones on dry ground. They steal stones from each other!

The females each lay two eggs. Both parents take turns to sit on the eggs to keep them warm.

When the chicks hatch, their parents are kept busy catching fish and krill for them.

Male emperor penguins spend the winter on the Antarctic pack ice.

First one parent, and then the other, hurries from the nest to the sea and back again. It is often a long walk. Penguins in a hurry will sometimes lie on their fronts and toboggan over the snow.

The chicks need lots of food and they grow very quickly.

They stay close to their parents who try to protect them from summer blizzards and the attacks of skuas (see page 14).

When do Adélie penguins build their nests?

Penguins' enemies

Large gulls called skuas often nest near Adélie penguins. Skuas are scavengers, and they eat broken eggs and dead chicks. This keeps the penguin rookeries clean. But skuas are always on the lookout for eggs to steal, and they kill stray penguin chicks if they can.

Skuas

Adélie penguins build their nests in summer.

Leopard seal

Leopard seals are a worse danger to penguins. The seals lurk in the sea near penguin rookeries. They know they can catch some of the hundreds of penguins that dive into the sea to get food. But penguins can twist and turn and dodge, and sometimes they escape by leaping high onto rocks.

Orca (or killer) whales hunt penguins, too.

Which seals lurk in the sea near penguin rookeries?

Where emperor and Adélie penguins live

Long lines of penguins trek across the snow and ice of the Antarctic. Every year they come ashore to lay their eggs and raise their chicks.

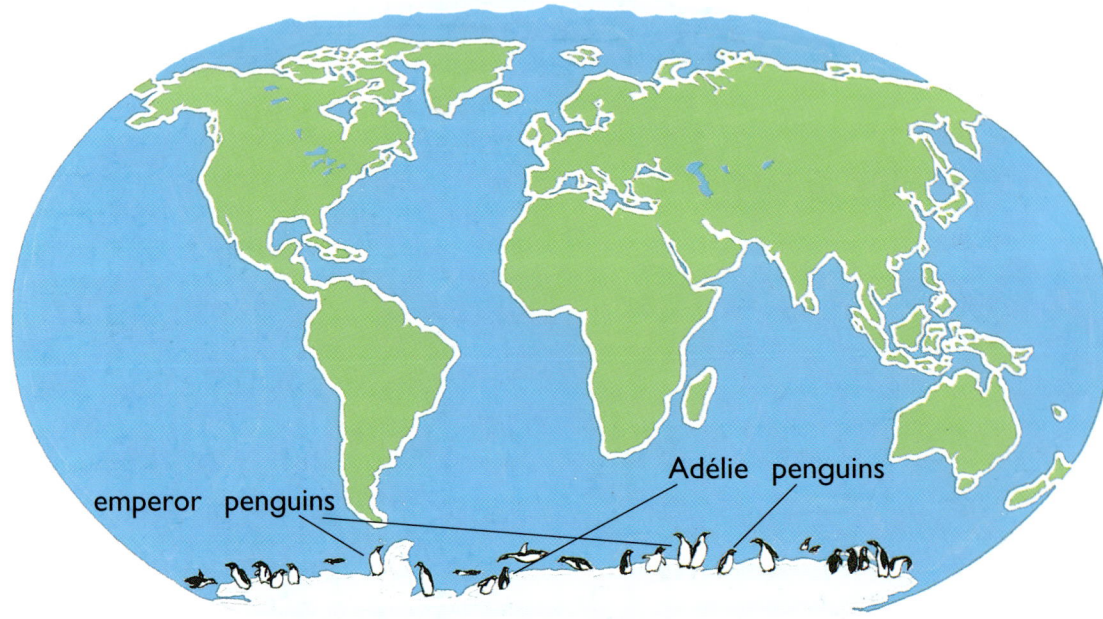

Leopard seals lurk in the sea near penguin rookeries.